SPACECRAFT

Written by Ian Graham
Illustrated by Roger Stewart

RSVP
RAINTREE
STECK-VAUGHN
PUBLISHERS
The Steck-Vaughn Company

Austin, Texas

Editor: Dr. Skipp Tullen
Project Manager: Julie Klaus

Library of Congress Cataloging-in-Publication Data
Graham, Ian, 1953-
     Spacecraft / written by Ian Graham; illustrated by Roger Stewart.
       p.   cm. — (Pointers)
     Includes index.
     ISBN 0-8114-6193-9
     1. Space vehicles — History — Juvenile literature. [1. Space vehicles — History.] I. Stewart, Roger, ill. II. Title. III. Series.
TL793.G687 1995
629.4—dc20   94-2875
                                                 CIP
                                               AC

Printed and bound in the United States

1 2 3 4 5 6 7 8 9 0 VH 99 98 97 96 95 94

Foreword

This book is about different types of spacecraft. All of them have certain things in common. For example, they are all launched by rockets, and they all carry scientific instruments and radio equipment. They have to be strong enough to withstand great stress, such as vibration during liftoff and both roasting and freezing temperatures. Spacecraft operated by humans must also have life-support systems so their crews can survive in space.

Each spacecraft is also very different. Each is designed for a different job. Early spacecraft proved that spaceflight was possible. The first human-operated space capsules proved that people could survive in space. Since then, satellites with special functions have been launched. They relay telephone calls and TV pictures between continents, photograph weather systems, and search for minerals.

Deep space probes have visited other planets in the solar system. Astronauts have landed on the moon and flown into space in reusable space shuttles. And people have lived in space for months at a time in space stations. This book looks at all these different types of spacecraft to find out what makes each one of them special.

Contents

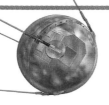

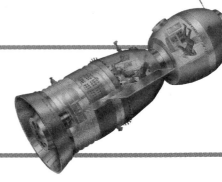

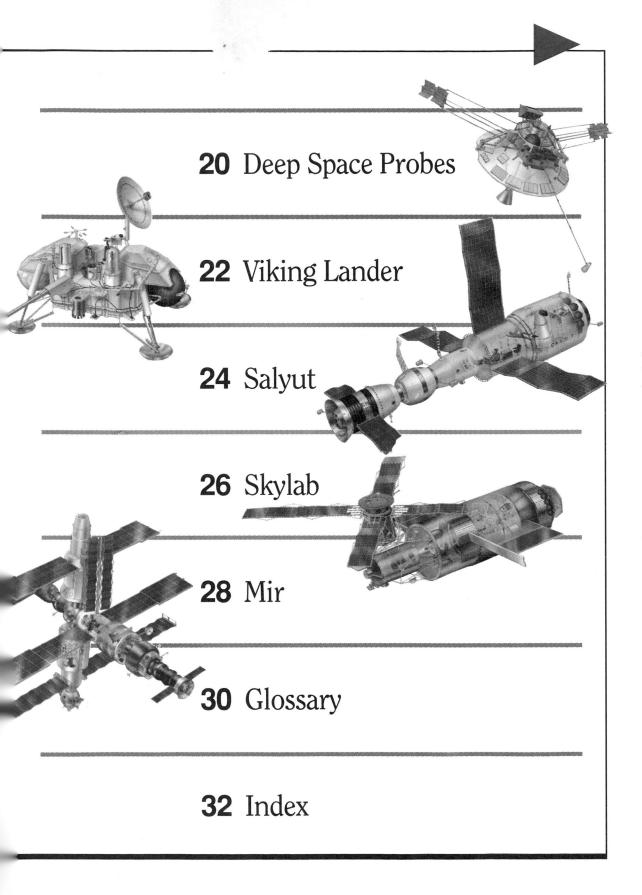

► Early Satellites

The Space Age began on October 4, 1957 when the Soviet Union launched *Sputnik 1*, the first artificial satellite. It was a steel sphere 23 inches (58 cm) across, containing a radio transmitter.

   Sputnik 2, launched on November 3, 1957, carried the first living creature into space — a dog named Laika. Then on January 31, 1958, the United States launched its first satellite, *Explorer 1*. These first satellites proved that space technology really worked. The next step was to put people in space.

Explorer 1

▼ 2

Sputnik 1

2 Four flexible whip antennae, which varied in length from 5 feet (1.5 m) to nearly 10 feet (3 m), transmitted radio signals to Earth from *Sputnik 1*.

Antennae

1 The radio transmitter on *Sputnik 1* sent signals for 21 days. The way these signals changed on their way to Earth gave useful information about the Earth's atmosphere.

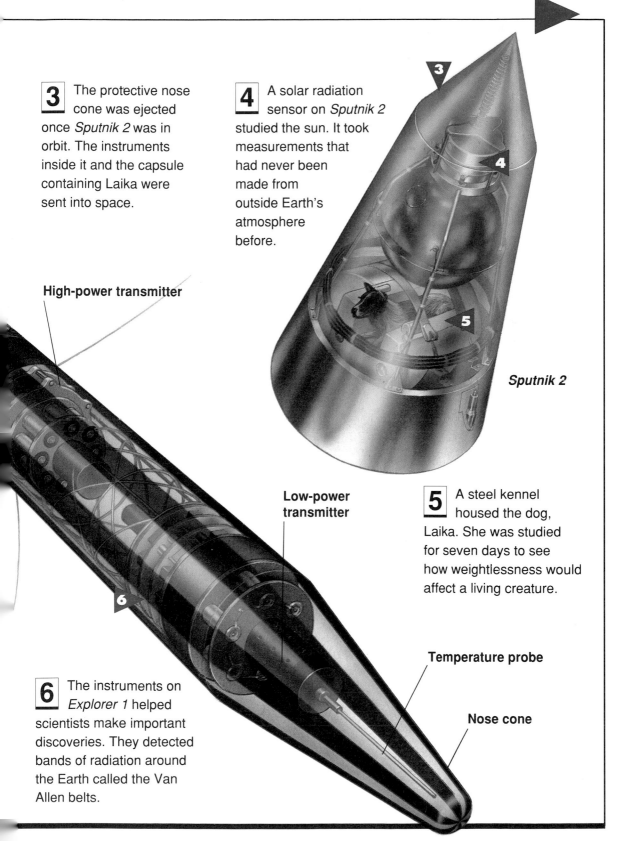

3 The protective nose cone was ejected once *Sputnik 2* was in orbit. The instruments inside it and the capsule containing Laika were sent into space.

4 A solar radiation sensor on *Sputnik 2* studied the sun. It took measurements that had never been made from outside Earth's atmosphere before.

High-power transmitter

Sputnik 2

Low-power transmitter

5 A steel kennel housed the dog, Laika. She was studied for seven days to see how weightlessness would affect a living creature.

Temperature probe

6 The instruments on *Explorer 1* helped scientists make important discoveries. They detected bands of radiation around the Earth called the Van Allen belts.

Nose cone

Space Capsules

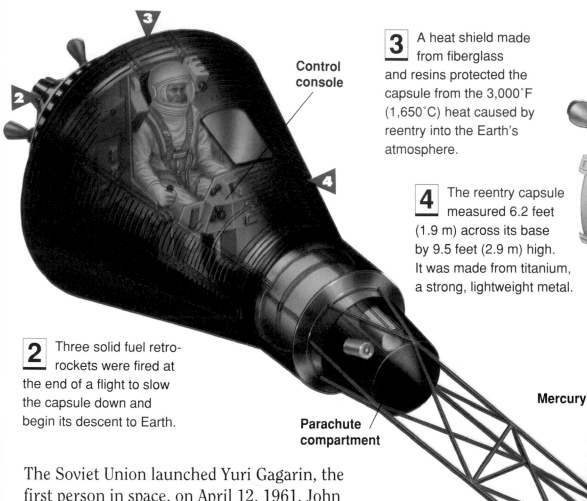

3 A heat shield made from fiberglass and resins protected the capsule from the 3,000°F (1,650°C) heat caused by reentry into the Earth's atmosphere.

4 The reentry capsule measured 6.2 feet (1.9 m) across its base by 9.5 feet (2.9 m) high. It was made from titanium, a strong, lightweight metal.

Control console

2 Three solid fuel retro-rockets were fired at the end of a flight to slow the capsule down and begin its descent to Earth.

Mercury

Parachute compartment

The Soviet Union launched Yuri Gagarin, the first person in space, on April 12, 1961. John Glenn became the first American astronaut to orbit the Earth on February 20, 1962. Each man was sealed inside a simple metal capsule launched by rockets. In space, the capsules changed course by firing small rocket thrusters. The American Mercury capsule was designed to be flown by the astronaut, but the Soviet Vostok capsule was controlled from Earth. Both capsules had heat shields to protect them from the high temperatures caused by friction between the capsule and the air as they reentered Earth's atmosphere.

1 A launch escape tower was attached to the nose of the capsule. It had its own solid-fuel rocket with three angled nozzles. If the astronaut was in danger during lift-off, the rocket could blast the capsule safely away.

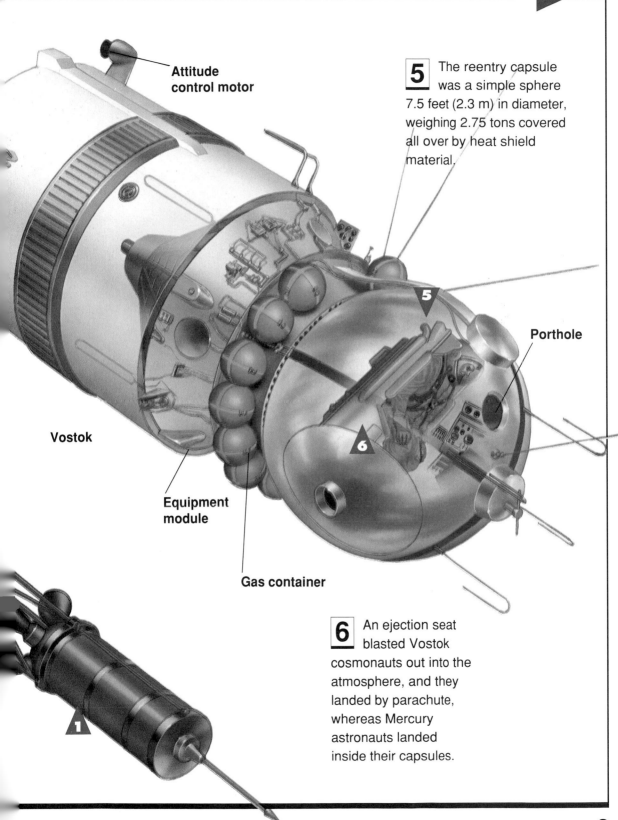

Attitude
control motor

5 The reentry capsule
was a simple sphere
7.5 feet (2.3 m) in diameter,
weighing 2.75 tons covered
all over by heat shield
material.

5

Porthole

Vostok

6

Equipment
module

Gas container

6 An ejection seat
blasted Vostok
cosmonauts out into the
atmosphere, and they
landed by parachute,
whereas Mercury
astronauts landed
inside their capsules.

1

Gemini

Gemini spacecraft were used by the United States in the next stage of space exploration. They were two-person spacecraft, larger than Mercury, and, at 4.2 tons, double the weight. Gemini spacecraft were designed to try out the techniques that would be needed for flights to the moon in later years. The astronauts docked (linked) their spacecraft with rockets in Earth orbit. They opened the hatches and floated into space at the end of ropelike tethers. The Gemini spacecraft also carried the first computer used in space.

4 Sixteen steering thrusters in the equipment module and retro-module enabled Gemini astronauts to steer their spacecraft while in orbit.

3 Gemini's reentry module looked like an enlarged Mercury capsule. Before reentry, the equipment module and retro-module were detached and discarded.

2 Radar equipment in the nose was used to detect other rockets and spacecraft so that Gemini could meet and dock with them.

1 Reentry thrusters in the nose section steered the spacecraft as it plunged back to Earth through the atmosphere.

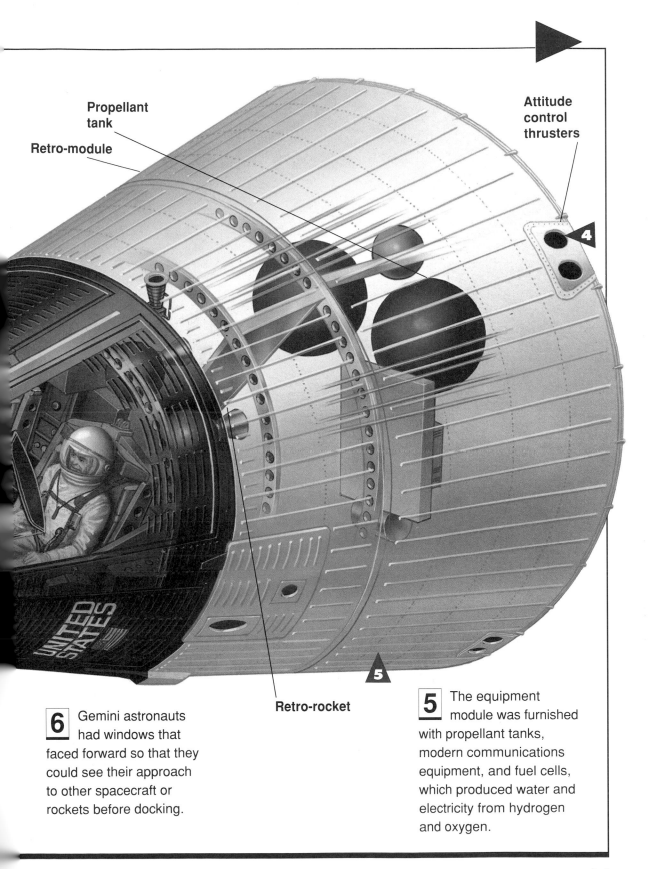

Propellant tank

Retro-module

Attitude control thrusters

4

5

Retro-rocket

6 Gemini astronauts had windows that faced forward so that they could see their approach to other spacecraft or rockets before docking.

5 The equipment module was furnished with propellant tanks, modern communications equipment, and fuel cells, which produced water and electricity from hydrogen and oxygen.

UNITED STATES

Apollo

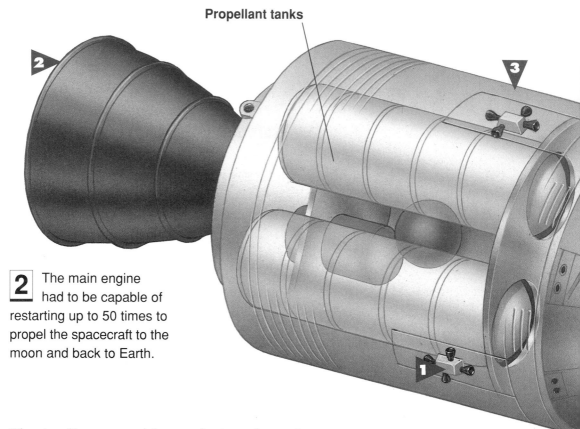

Propellant tanks

2 The main engine had to be capable of restarting up to 50 times to propel the spacecraft to the moon and back to Earth.

The Apollo spacecraft was designed to take astronauts to the moon. It consisted of two main parts: the command and service module (CSM) and the lunar excursion module (LEM). After launch by a massive *Saturn V* rocket, the CSM and LEM flew to the moon. In lunar orbit they separated, and the LEM landed two of the three astronauts on the moon. After a short stay, part of the LEM was relaunched from the moon's surface, carrying the astronauts up to rejoin the CSM in lunar orbit for the return journey. In seven flights between 1969 and 1972, Apollo astronauts brought 854 pounds (388 kg) of moon rocks back to Earth.

1 Apollo had four quad thrusters, each with four rockets pointing in different directions, on the CSM. Astronauts used them to move the module in any direction with great precision.

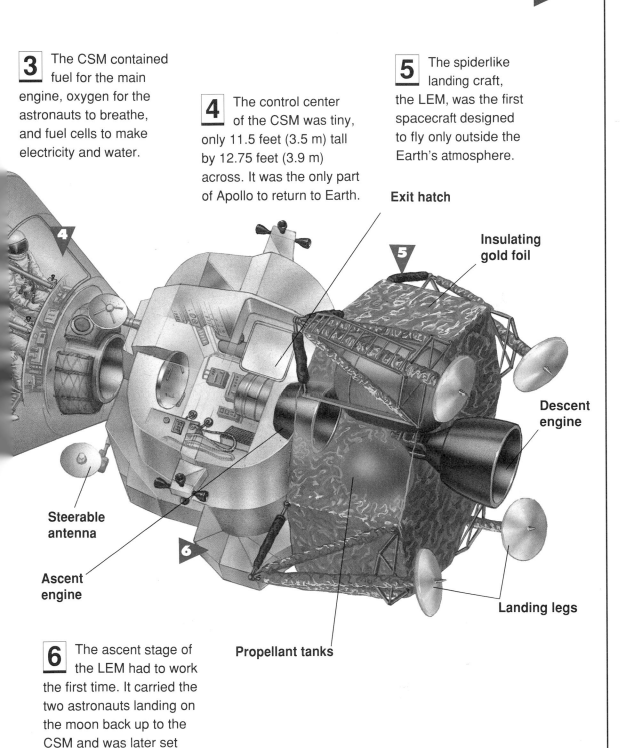

3 The CSM contained fuel for the main engine, oxygen for the astronauts to breathe, and fuel cells to make electricity and water.

4 The control center of the CSM was tiny, only 11.5 feet (3.5 m) tall by 12.75 feet (3.9 m) across. It was the only part of Apollo to return to Earth.

5 The spiderlike landing craft, the LEM, was the first spacecraft designed to fly only outside the Earth's atmosphere.

Exit hatch

Insulating gold foil

Descent engine

Steerable antenna

Ascent engine

Landing legs

Propellant tanks

6 The ascent stage of the LEM had to work the first time. It carried the two astronauts landing on the moon back up to the CSM and was later set adrift.

Soyuz

In the 1960s the Soviet Union developed a new spacecraft called Soyuz, meaning "union." It could carry a crew of one, two, or three. It was divided into three sections — a command or reentry module in the middle (the only part to return to Earth), an equipment module at one end, and an orbital module at the other.

Electrical power was supplied by a pair of solar panels. The first Soyuz operated from space by humans was launched on April 23, 1967. Soyuz spacecraft were used to ferry crews to and from the Salyut space station, and they are still used to carry crews to the *Mir* space station.

2 Two winglike solar panels unfold from the sides of the equipment module to make electricity from sunlight.

Retro-rocket

1 The Soyuz equipment module houses small rockets for steering and larger rockets that slow Soyuz down for reentry and landing.

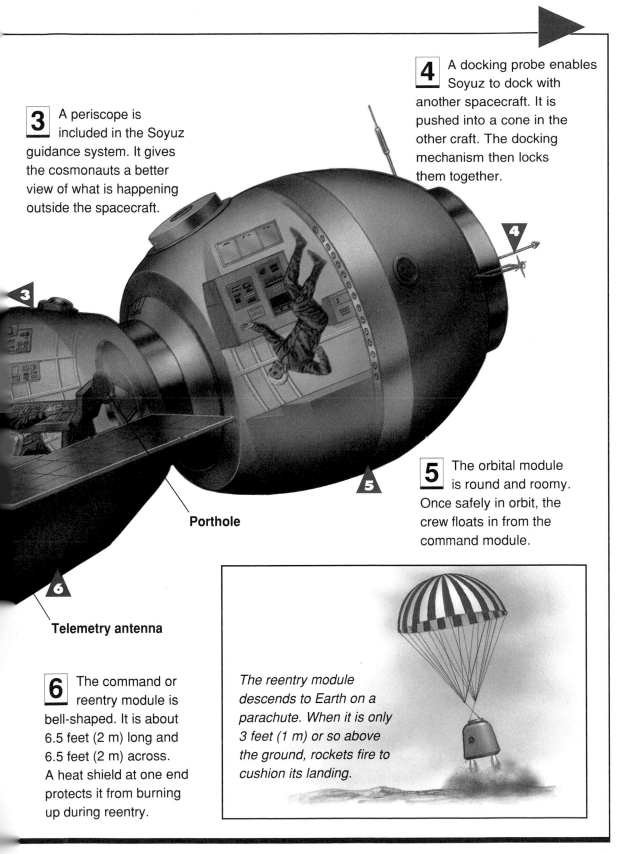

3 A periscope is included in the Soyuz guidance system. It gives the cosmonauts a better view of what is happening outside the spacecraft.

4 A docking probe enables Soyuz to dock with another spacecraft. It is pushed into a cone in the other craft. The docking mechanism then locks them together.

Porthole

5 The orbital module is round and roomy. Once safely in orbit, the crew floats in from the command module.

Telemetry antenna

6 The command or reentry module is bell-shaped. It is about 6.5 feet (2 m) long and 6.5 feet (2 m) across. A heat shield at one end protects it from burning up during reentry.

The reentry module descends to Earth on a parachute. When it is only 3 feet (1 m) or so above the ground, rockets fire to cushion its landing.

Space Shuttle

For the first 24 years of the Space Age, every rocket, satellite, probe, and spacecraft operated by humans was used only once. The space shuttle is the first of a new type of spacecraft that can be used again and again. It has three main parts: the orbiter, an external fuel tank, and two booster rockets. The orbiter carries satellites into space in a compartment called a payload bay. The boosters provide extra thrust to help launch the shuttle. The external tank supplies fuel to the orbiter's engines during liftoff. The boosters and the orbiter are reused, but a new external tank is needed for each flight.

3 The payload bay on the orbiter can carry up to 32 tons of cargo into space, usually satellites and scientific instruments. The bay measures 61 feet (18.5 m) long by 15 feet (4.5 m) across.

Rudder

Orbital maneuvering system (OMS) engine

2 A cluster of three rocket engines in the orbiter's tail provides the main propulsion for liftoff. They burn 1,060 gallons (4,000 liters) of liquid hydrogen and oxygen from the external tank every second. The power of the engines can be varied, and they also swivel to steer the spacecraft.

1 The 147-foot- (45-m-) long booster rockets are the first solid fuel rockets used on a spacecraft operated by humans and the largest yet used in spaceflight.

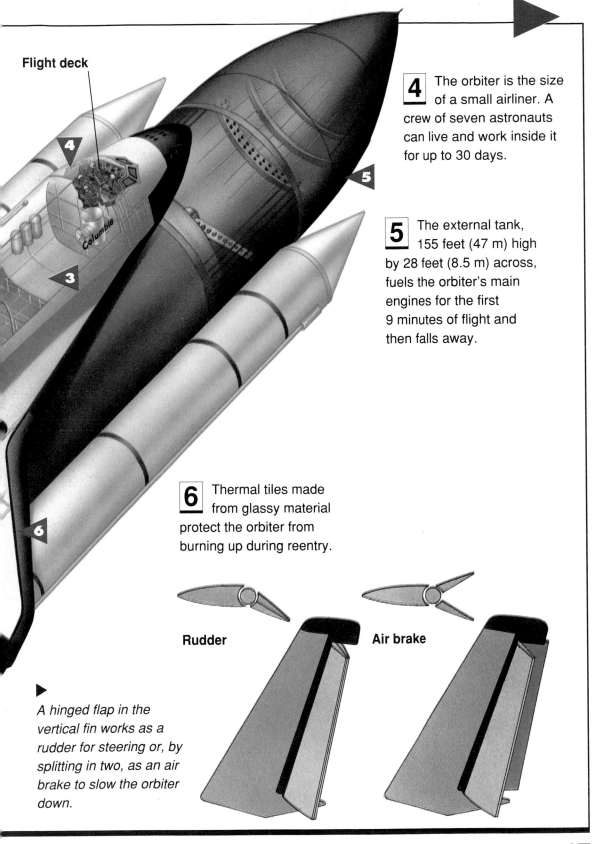

Flight deck

4 The orbiter is the size of a small airliner. A crew of seven astronauts can live and work inside it for up to 30 days.

5 The external tank, 155 feet (47 m) high by 28 feet (8.5 m) across, fuels the orbiter's main engines for the first 9 minutes of flight and then falls away.

6 Thermal tiles made from glassy material protect the orbiter from burning up during reentry.

Rudder

Air brake

▶ *A hinged flap in the vertical fin works as a rudder for steering or, by splitting in two, as an air brake to slow the orbiter down.*

Modern Satellites

Satellites in orbit around the Earth help us in many ways. Communications satellites relay information around the world. Scientific satellites study the stars. Weather satellites provide meteorologists with photographs of weather systems. Earth resources satellites monitor changes in the Earth's environment and help to find valuable minerals. Navigation satellites help to guide ships and aircraft. They all produce electrical power for their instruments by means of solar panels, and they also have small thrusters to keep their instruments and antennae pointing in the right direction.

2 The synthetic aperture radar system uses electronics to amplify the signals from the 33-foot- (10-m-) long antenna and provide clearer pictures of the ground.

Wind data antenna

Radar altimeter antenna

***ERS 1* (Earth resources satellite)**

Payload electronics module

1 A laser retro-reflector bounces back a laser beam sent from Earth to check on the satellite's position in space.

Radiometer

Solar panels

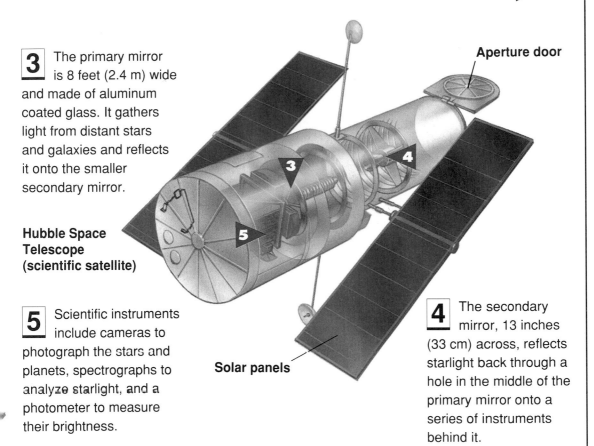

3 The primary mirror is 8 feet (2.4 m) wide and made of aluminum coated glass. It gathers light from distant stars and galaxies and reflects it onto the smaller secondary mirror.

Aperture door

Hubble Space Telescope (scientific satellite)

Solar panels

5 Scientific instruments include cameras to photograph the stars and planets, spectrographs to analyze starlight, and a photometer to measure their brightness.

4 The secondary mirror, 13 inches (33 cm) across, reflects starlight back through a hole in the middle of the primary mirror onto a series of instruments behind it.

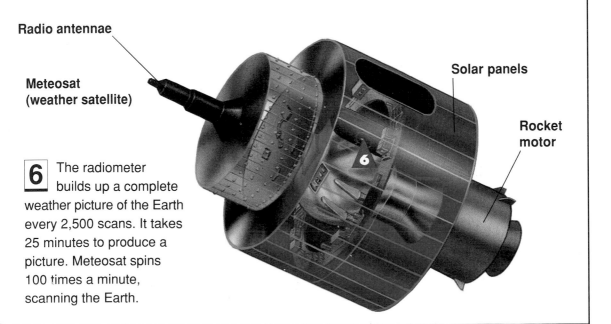

Radio antennae

Meteosat (weather satellite)

Solar panels

Rocket motor

6 The radiometer builds up a complete weather picture of the Earth every 2,500 scans. It takes 25 minutes to produce a picture. Meteosat spins 100 times a minute, scanning the Earth.

Deep Space Probes

Deep space probes travel millions of miles to collect information about the sun and the planets and send it back to Earth. The first deep space probe, *Luna 1*, was boosted out of Earth's orbit toward the moon in 1959. Since then, deep space probes have flown by every planet in the solar system except Pluto. The Pioneer probes visited the moon, Venus, Jupiter, and Saturn. In 1986, the European probe *Giotto* took close-up photographs of Halley's Comet from only 368 miles (596 km) away. The most successful probes were the Voyagers, which toured the planets for 12 years in the 1970s and 1980s.

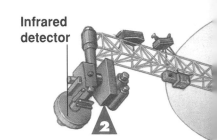

Infrared detector

2 A scan platform carried *Voyager's* TV cameras and some of its instruments. The platform could be pointed in any direction.

1 A two-layer bumper shield on *Giotto* protected the instruments from dust particles, which flew into it at 50 times the speed of a bullet.

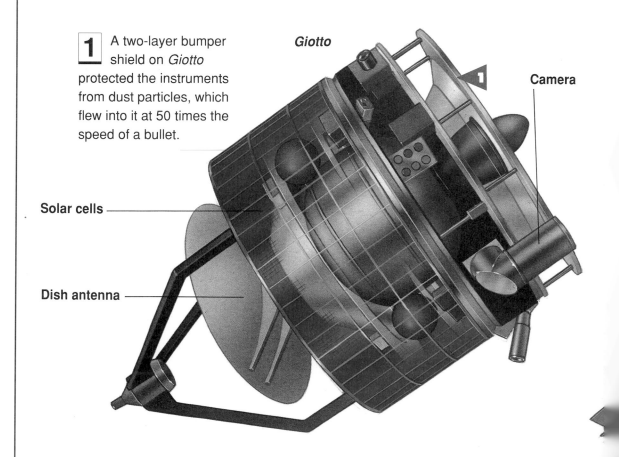

Giotto

Camera

Solar cells

Dish antenna

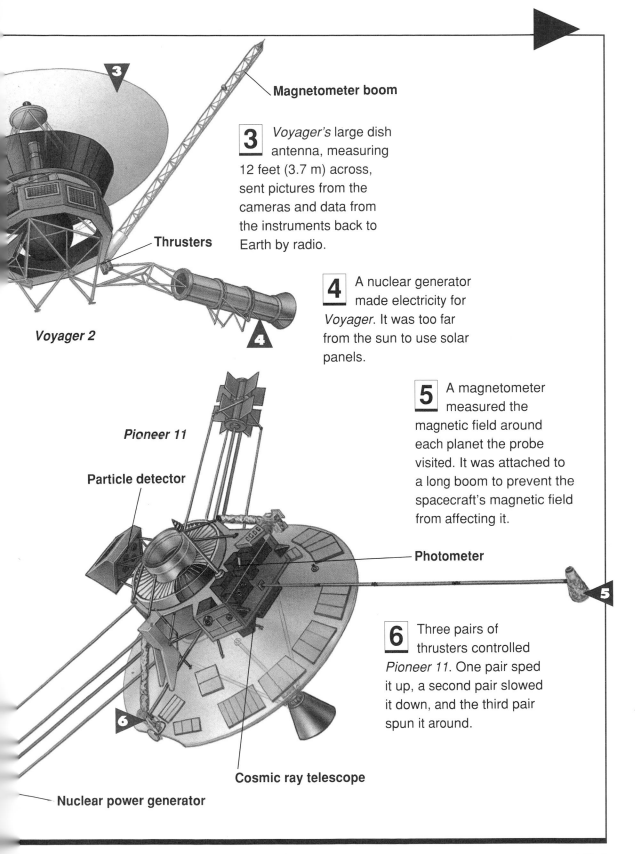

Magnetometer boom

3 *Voyager's* large dish antenna, measuring 12 feet (3.7 m) across, sent pictures from the cameras and data from the instruments back to Earth by radio.

Thrusters

Voyager 2

4 A nuclear generator made electricity for *Voyager*. It was too far from the sun to use solar panels.

5 A magnetometer measured the magnetic field around each planet the probe visited. It was attached to a long boom to prevent the spacecraft's magnetic field from affecting it.

Pioneer 11

Particle detector

Photometer

6 Three pairs of thrusters controlled *Pioneer 11*. One pair sped it up, a second pair slowed it down, and the third pair spun it around.

Cosmic ray telescope

Nuclear power generator

Viking Lander

Landing craft, or landers, are spacecraft designed to make a soft landing on the moon or planets and then continue transmitting information afterward. The first spacecraft to visit the moon was intentionally crash landed. The Soviet Union was very successful with a series of landers on the planet Venus. Then in the 1970s the United States sent two Viking spacecraft to Mars to study the planet and look for signs of life. Once a Viking craft reached Martian orbit, it separated into an orbiter, which remained in space, and a lander, which descended to the planet's surface.

3 A test card carrying a set of known colors was placed within view of Viking's two cameras to check that the photographs it took showed true colors.

Radio antennae

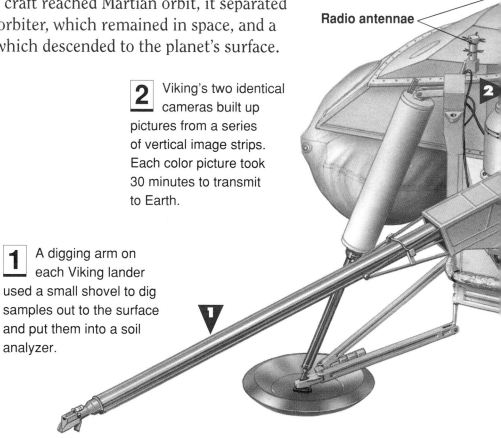

2 Viking's two identical cameras built up pictures from a series of vertical image strips. Each color picture took 30 minutes to transmit to Earth.

1 A digging arm on each Viking lander used a small shovel to dig samples out to the surface and put them into a soil analyzer.

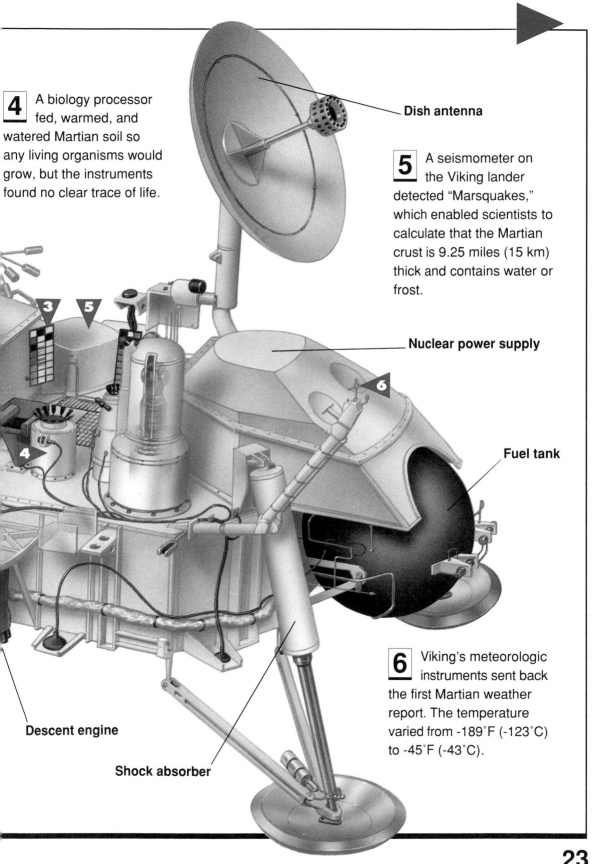

4 A biology processor fed, warmed, and watered Martian soil so any living organisms would grow, but the instruments found no clear trace of life.

Dish antenna

5 A seismometer on the Viking lander detected "Marsquakes," which enabled scientists to calculate that the Martian crust is 9.25 miles (15 km) thick and contains water or frost.

Nuclear power supply

Fuel tank

Descent engine

Shock absorber

6 Viking's meteorologic instruments sent back the first Martian weather report. The temperature varied from -189°F (-123°C) to -45°F (-43°C).

Salyut

In the 1970s and 1980s, the Soviet Union launched seven Salyut ("salute") space stations. *Salyut 4* was 76 feet (23 m) long and weighed 20.5 tons. It circled the Earth every 89 minutes at a height of 135-167 miles (219-270 km). It was launched in 1974 and stayed in orbit until it reentered the atmosphere in 1977. Salyut's cosmonauts carried out thousands of scientific experiments and photographed millions of square miles of the Earth's surface. Salyut gave the Soviet Union information on the unique experience of long spaceflights and their effects on the human body.

3 Salyut's air lock compartment, which was 10 feet (3 m) long by 6 feet (2 m) across, allowed cosmonauts to enter and leave the Salyut space station safely. The small dish antenna on the tall tower is part of Salyut's navigation system.

2 A Soyuz spacecraft ferried crews to and from Salyut. Later Soyuz ferries were powered by batteries instead of solar panels.

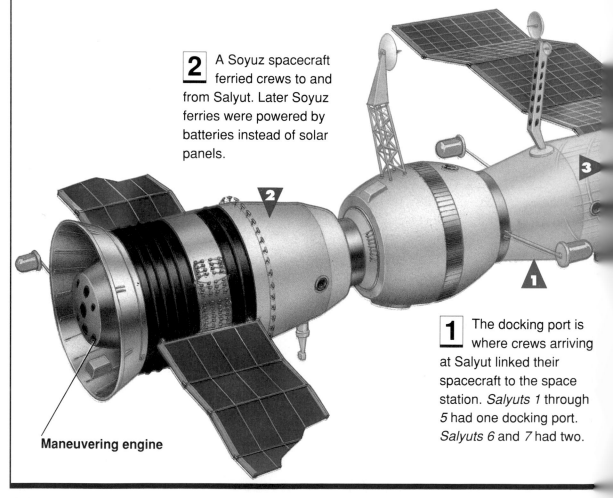

Maneuvering engine

1 The docking port is where crews arriving at Salyut linked their spacecraft to the space station. *Salyuts 1* through *5* had one docking port. *Salyuts 6* and *7* had two.

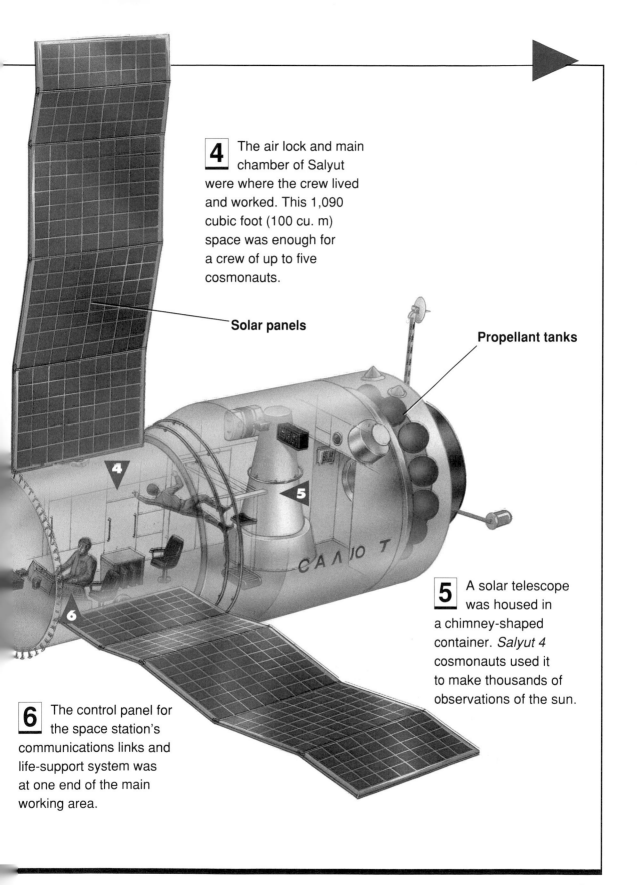

4 The air lock and main chamber of Salyut were where the crew lived and worked. This 1,090 cubic foot (100 cu. m) space was enough for a crew of up to five cosmonauts.

Solar panels

Propellant tanks

5 A solar telescope was housed in a chimney-shaped container. *Salyut 4* cosmonauts used it to make thousands of observations of the sun.

6 The control panel for the space station's communications links and life-support system was at one end of the main working area.

Skylab

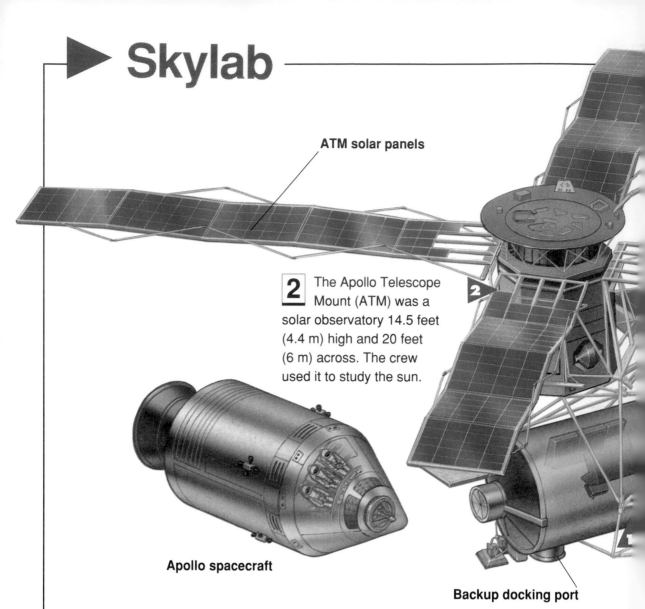

ATM solar panels

2 The Apollo Telescope Mount (ATM) was a solar observatory 14.5 feet (4.4 m) high and 20 feet (6 m) across. The crew used it to study the sun.

Apollo spacecraft

Backup docking port

In 1973, the United States launched its *Skylab* space station, made partly from leftover Apollo spacecraft. Part of *Skylab* was made from a fuel tank from a *Saturn V* rocket. Its three-person crews were ferried to and from orbit by Apollo spacecraft. Despite suffering serious damage during liftoff, *Skylab* was a great success. Its astronauts welded metals, grew crystals, and took thousands of pictures of the Earth and sun. *Skylab* was destroyed when it reentered Earth's atmosphere in 1979.

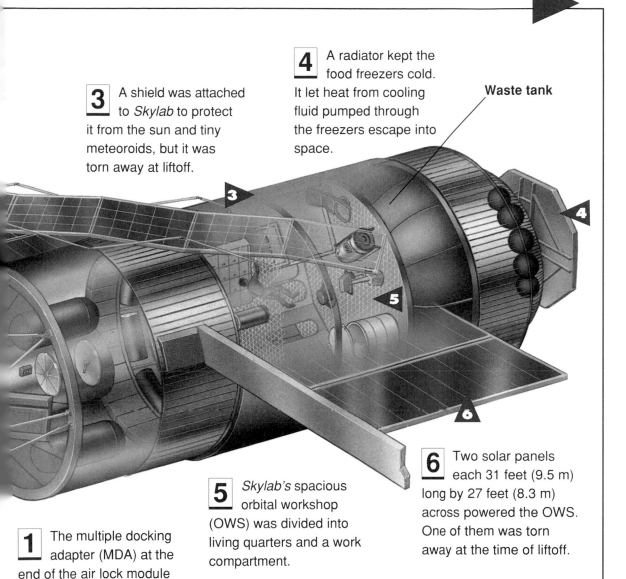

3 A shield was attached to *Skylab* to protect it from the sun and tiny meteoroids, but it was torn away at liftoff.

4 A radiator kept the food freezers cold. It let heat from cooling fluid pumped through the freezers escape into space.

Waste tank

5 *Skylab's* spacious orbital workshop (OWS) was divided into living quarters and a work compartment.

6 Two solar panels each 31 feet (9.5 m) long by 27 feet (8.3 m) across powered the OWS. One of them was torn away at the time of liftoff.

1 The multiple docking adapter (MDA) at the end of the air lock module allowed astronauts to enter and leave *Skylab*. The MDA contained two docking ports — the main port in the end and a backup in the side.

To protect Skylab *from overheating after its sun shield was torn off during liftoff, astronauts put a new sunshade over it.*

Mir

In 1986, the Soviet Union launched a new type of space station called *Mir* (pronounced "meer"), meaning "peace." It was larger than Salyut and built with six docking ports instead of Salyut's two ports. These enabled the space station to be expanded by linking more modules to the base unit. Two Kvant modules and a *Kristall* module were added in 1987, 1989, and 1990. *Mir* is still in orbit. Two more modules, *Spektr* and *Priroda*, may be added in the future. A new base unit, *Mir 2*, may be added, too, taking over control of the complex from *Mir 1*, which will remain in place. An American space shuttle is due to dock with *Mir* in 1995.

4 The *Kvant 2* module is a large cylinder, 45 feet (13.7 m) long, containing a laboratory where the cosmonauts can carry out scientific experiments.

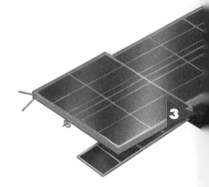

3 Progress spacecraft bring mail and fuel, food, water, and air to re-supply *Mir*. Their engines are also used to adjust *Mir's* position.

2 The multiple docking adapter on *Mir's* base unit has five docking ports, and a sixth is at the other end of the station.

1 The *Kristall* module is a mini-factory in space, powered by solar panels. It is designed to manufacture ultra-pure medicines and flawless crystals for making computer chips.

Extra docking port ___

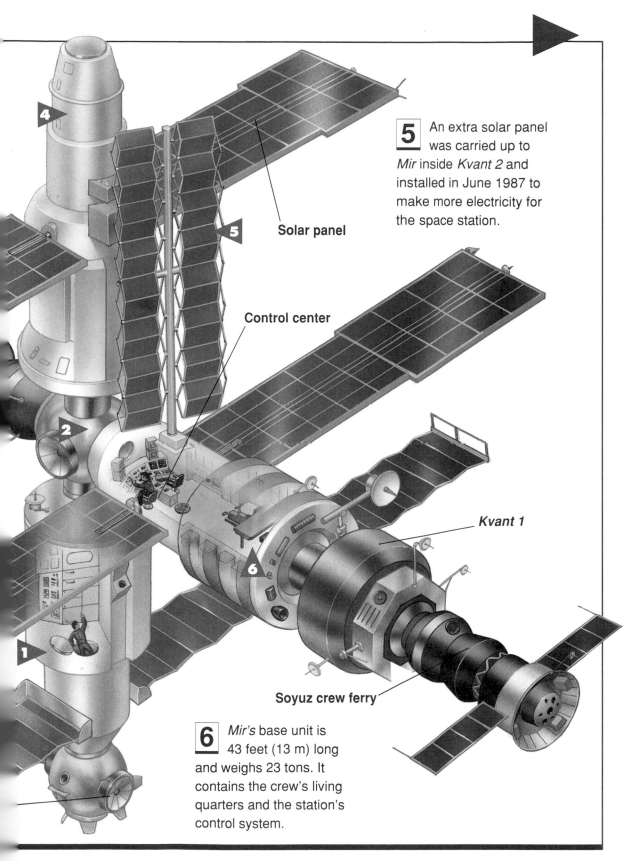

5 An extra solar panel was carried up to *Mir* inside *Kvant 2* and installed in June 1987 to make more electricity for the space station.

Solar panel

Control center

Kvant 1

Soyuz crew ferry

6 *Mir's* base unit is 43 feet (13 m) long and weighs 23 tons. It contains the crew's living quarters and the station's control system.

▶ Glossary

Air brake
A hinged flap on an aircraft or space shuttle designed to slow the craft down

Air lock
A compartment with an airtight door at each end to enable the crew to enter and leave without all the air in the craft escaping

Altimeter
An instrument that measures a craft's height above the ground

Altitude
The height of an aircraft or spacecraft above the ground

Aperture
An opening. A telescope's aperture lets in light.

Astronaut
Someone trained for space travel

Atmosphere
The gases that surround the Earth or any other planet

Attitude
The position of a craft in space

Boom
A long thin pole used to hold a sensitive instrument away from a satellite

Booster
A rocket that provides additional thrust for liftoff

Capsule
A simple spacecraft consisting of a single sealed compartment

Comet
A lump of ice and dust circling the sun with an oval orbit that takes it far out of sight of the Earth for many years at a time

Cosmonaut
The Russian word for astronaut

Docking
Linking two or more spacecraft together

Flight deck
A spacecraft's control compartment

Friction
A force that slows down an object by rubbing it against another, as when air rubs against a descending spacecraft

Fuel cell
A device which makes electricity by combining hydrogen and oxygen gases. Pure water is also produced.

Galaxies
Enormous groups of stars traveling together through space. Each contains roughly one hundred billion stars.

Hatch
An airtight door in a spacecraft

Heat shield
The part of a spacecraft that protects it from burning up when it reenters the atmosphere

Laser
An instrument that produces an intense beam of light

Lunar
Relating to the moon

Meteoroid
A tiny speck of matter traveling through space

Meteorology
The scientific study of the atmosphere and weather

Module
One complete part of a spacecraft that can separate from another

Orbit
The path of a satellite around a planet or star

Payload
The cargo carried by a spacecraft

Periscope
An optical instrument allowing the viewer to see objects not in the direct line of vision

Photometer
An instrument used to measure light intensity

Planet
A large body in orbit around a sun

Port
An opening in a spacecraft where another spacecraft may dock

Porthole
A window, usually circular, in the side of a spacecraft

Propellant
The fuel used to propel a rocket or spacecraft

Propulsion
The pushing of a rocket or spacecraft forward

Quad thruster
A set of four thrusters

Radiometer
An instrument for measuring any kind of electromagnetic energy

Retro-module
Part of the spacecraft that contains the retro-rockets

Retroreflector
A reflector that sends light back the way it came

Retro-rocket
A rocket that slows down a spacecraft to begin its descent

Satellite
An object in orbit around a planet

Seismometer
An instrument for detecting and measuring earthquakes

Solar panel
Panels of special cells that produce electricity from sunlight

Space station
A base in space, where astronauts live and work for months at a time

Spectrograph
An instrument for analyzing light for its component colors

Stage
A section of a rocket with its own motor or motors

Telemetry
The transmission of information about a spacecraft to the ground control center automatically by radio

Telescope
An instrument which gives an enlarged view of distant objects

Tether
A ropelike safety line connecting an astronaut floating in space to the spacecraft

Thruster
A small rocket engine used for steering a spacecraft or satellite

Ton
2,000 pounds

►Index

air brake 17
air lock 24
antenna 6, 18, 20
Apollo 12–13
astronaut 8, 10, 11, 12, 13, 17, 26, 27
atmosphere 6, 7

battery 24
booster rocket 16

camera 19, 20, 21, 22
capsule 8, 9
communications equipment 11, 25
communications satellite 18
computer 10
cosmonaut 9, 15, 24, 25, 28

docking 10, 15
docking port 24, 26, 28
docking probe 15

ejection seat 9
electricity 11, 13, 14, 18, 29
ERS 1 (Earth resources satellite) 18
Explorer 1 6

flight deck 17
fuel 13, 16
fuel cell 11, 13
fuel tank 16

Gagarin, Yuri 8
Gemini 10–11
Giotto 20
Glenn, John 8

Halley's Comet 20
heat shield 8, 9, 15
Hubble Space Telescope 19
hydrogen 11, 16

infrared detector 20

Jupiter 20

laboratory 28

Laika 6, 7
landing craft 22–23
laser 18
launch escape tower 8
life-support system 25
liftoff 16
Luna 1 20
lunar excursion module (LEM) 12, 13
lunar orbit 12

magnetometer 21
Mars 22
Mercury 8
meteoroid 27
meteorology 18, 19, 23
Meteosat 19
mineral 18
Mir 14, 28–29
mirror 19
moon 12, 13, 20, 22
moon rock 12
multiple docking adapter (MDA) 27, 28

navigation satellite 18

orbital workshop (OWS) 27
oxygen 11, 13, 16

parachute 9, 15
payload bay 16
periscope 15
photograph 24, 26
photometer 19
Pioneer 11 21
planet 20
probes 20, 21
Progress 28
propellant tanks 11, 12, 25

quad thruster 12

radar 10
radio 6
radiometer 18
reentry 8, 14, 15
rocket,
    booster 16

retro- 8, 14
    solid fuel 16
    steering 14
rocket thruster 8
rudder 16, 17

Salyut 14, 24–25, 28
Salyut 4 24–25
satellite 6, 16, 18–19
Saturn 20
Saturn V 12, 26
scientific instrument 7, 16
scientific satellite 18, 19
seismometer 23
Skylab 26–27
soil 22, 23
solar observatory 25, 26
solar panel 14, 18, 19, 25, 27, 29
solar system 20
Soyuz 14, 15, 24
space shuttle 16–17
space station 24–25, 26–27, 28–29
spectrograph 19
Sputnik 1 6
Sputnik 2 6, 7
sun 26
sun shield 27

telemetry 15
thermal tile 17
thruster 8, 10, 12, 21
titanium 8
TV camera 20

Van Allen belt 7
Venus 20, 22
Viking 22
Viking lander 22–23
Vostok 9
Voyager 20
Voyager 2 21

water 13
weather satellite 18, 19
weightlessness 7

© 1994 Andromeda Oxford Limited

DATE DUE

629.47   Graham, Ian.
GRA
          Spacecraft